LESSONS LEARNED FROM OUR MISSTAKES

Michael Rosman

www.TheCorporateCaterer.com

Copyright © 2015 Michael Rosman
All rights reserved.
ISBN: 0692385991
ISBN-13: 978-0692385999 (The Corporate Caterer)

DEDICATION

This book is dedicated to the Greatest Caterer on Planet Earth, my wife Marcia.

I met Marcia in March 1997. At the time, she was (and still is), a partner and Director of Full-Service Catering at an independent company in suburban Boston that was seeking someone to build their corporate division. She interviewed and eventually hired me for the position.

Truth be told, I had a crush on her from day one.

The first three years we shared an office the size of a jail cell. One day, I mustered enough courage to ask if she "wanted to do something outside of work" over the upcoming weekend.

My recollection is her eyeing me up and down suspiciously, hesitating, and slowly saying, "I'll let you know tomorrow…" "Could have gone worse," I thought. "At least she didn't can me."

The next day she announced, "This is what I've decided. We can do something this weekend. BUT if anyone from work sees us, I lost a bet to you, and that's why we are out together."

"Ahh...ok" I stammered.

"And one more thing," she said. "You said we could do anything I want. I've thought about it. I want to go to Home Depot. I need a power drill."

That Sunday afternoon, we in fact did go to Home Depot. Afterwards, we went to Legal Sea Foods, sat up at the bar, and had appetizers and drinks.

Three months later I asked her to marry me. Six months later we tied the knot. In November 2015, we will have been married for fifteen years.

In addition to being my sounding board, editor, and moral compass, Marcia is the love of my life and my best friend.

PREFACE

If you operate a catering company, restaurant, franchise, corporate dining facility, food truck, or home catering business, *Lessons Learned From Our Misstakes* is a must-have for your professional library. Like many inexperienced operators, I had to figure out a lot through trial and error, especially in the early years.

Whether you are a novice in the world of corporate catering or a seasoned veteran, this book can help organize, manage, market, and grow your business. My hope is that my education at the School of Hard Knocks will offer systems to improve your efficiency, consistency, and service. Let my pain be your gain.

Hindsight can be a unique learning tool, especially when derived from the missteps of others. *Lessons Learned From Our Misstakes* contains about fifty real-life screw-ups, ill-conceived game plans, and wrong decisions (that felt right at the time), during my thirty plus years in the industry. And this is only Volume #1!

Most importantly, it shares the lessons learned from these experiences, and offers strategies that you can apply to your own operation.

In addition to all the "situations" presented, is a handful of true stories that have occurred over the years. These tales are a mixture of humor and pain that have served as growth opportunities and that I hope benefit you. (In some cases, names have been changed to protect the innocent.)

To sustain success, it's important to continuously move forward. Whether it's experimenting with new menu items, trying out-of-the box promotional concepts, offering innovative customer incentive programs, or doing something special for your employees, always consider your business a work in progress. Think of it as a journey, not a destination.

My official entry into the world of corporate catering was in the early 1990s. I owned a breakfast and lunch restaurant and later a pizzeria in the heart of Boston's financial district.

It didn't take long to realize that if I had any shot at success, I needed an additional revenue stream—and so began my corporate catering journey.

After about seven years of long days and hard work, my initial lease term on both restaurants were up for renewal. By then, I had realized that I could make more money, (and probably work fewer hours) by focusing exclusively on corporate catering.

The problem was that I was paying top-of-the-market rent for both restaurant locations. Signing new leases did not make sense. After some handwringing, I sold my catering client list to a large, independent competitor and took a six-month sabbatical.

When it was time to get back to work, I was offered the position of Director of Corporate Catering for an independent restaurant and caterer. The company was committed to building a corporate division, and the opportunity felt like a good fit. It became my home for the next sixteen years.

In 1998, corporate catering sales were $120,000.

By 2010, they were $1.8 million.

As of 2015, between both catering departments and the restaurant and bar (run by Marcia's partner, Al), our operation in Boston is on track to exceed $4.5 million annually in combined sales.

I recently asked Al how he felt about the fact that we had created one of the highest grossing, independently owned, single-unit operations in the region. In typical Al fashion, he responded, "How do I feel about it?...My feet hurt."

* * * * *

The forecast for the corporate catering sector is very encouraging. Not only do industry analysts agree that demand in this multi-billion dollar sector is on the rise and poised for continued growth, but that it is still a vastly under-tapped segment of the industry.

This is good news. It means there is a lot of business waiting to be captured. If you are looking for ways to boost your bottom line or generate a new revenue stream, corporate drop-off catering is your ticket.

THE CORPORATE CATERER
≈ Services Offered ≈

The Corporate Caterer is a company that evolved from my thirty plus years in the catering and restaurant business. We are a team of industry experts with in-the-trenches experience who want to share our knowledge and wisdom with you. Today, our success is measured by *your* future growth as a corporate drop-off caterer.

-Michael Rosman

1) Membership Website
Please visit www.TheCorporateCaterer.com for free downloads and information about our membership services. Our multi-media website shares behind-the-scenes trade tips, customizable templates and downloads, seasonal menus, sample sales scripts, and e-mails and letters for all situations in which you need help finding just the right words.

2) Coaching Membership
We offer one-to-one teleconferencing coaching memberships, which are available as weekly, biweekly, and monthly packages. For more details, visit www.TheCorporateCaterer.com and click the additional services link at the top of the homepage.

3) Custom Consulting

We conduct intensive, on-site consulting services at your locations(s). For more information, please call our corporate office to discuss your business goals at 781-641-3303

4) Leads Program

I am often asked if we "have lists?" We have created a pioneering leads program for members who want new business, but who don't have the time or staff for sales to be the priority that it should be.

This is how the Leads Program works:

- You give us zip codes where you want to pursue new business.

- Our specially trained, in-house lead generators make hundreds of cold calls on your behalf.

- You receive a confidential e-file of prequalified companies that regularly order catering and all their pertinent contact information. For more details, visit www.TheCorporateCaterer.com and click the additional services link at the top of the home page.

ACKNOWLEDGEMENTS

In *Lessons Learned From Our Misstakes*, I often use the pronoun "we" instead of "I." The reason is to acknowledge the literally hundreds of hard-working, talented people who have been part of my journey.

Successfully preparing and delivering fifty catering orders a day involves detailed planning, timely coordination from different departments of the operation, and the collective work of many people with various skill sets working in unison towards a common goal of delivering great food with a smile.

I sincerely thank my bosses early in my career who taught me how to be a better employee and all my employees who taught me how to be a better boss.

Finally, I'd like to thank three people whose wisdom and resources proved invaluable in creating **The Corporate Caterer.**

One is my financial advisor, Dick Sumberg. When I told Dick I was planning to launch new company—a membership website and coaching business for food service operators who aspire to grow a corporate drop-off catering division— he responded, "Figure out how much liquid capital you'll need to get it off the ground and err on the side of liberal. When you have a figure, and you're sure you've covered everything, *double it*. That's how much you will actually need."

"That's crazy," I thought. In time, I realized he was dead-on correct. Later, I learned he gives the same advice to all his clients, regardless of the venture. I share this because it could be an important rule of thumb in your own future endeavors.

Finally, I am extremely thankful to my parents, Syrille and Paul. In concert with Dick's accurate advice and without their belief in me, **The Corporate Caterer** would not have become a reality.

INTRODUCTION

From an early age, it was clear that Elise had found her calling. She was destined to take the catering industry by storm. By the time she was ten, she had established a sacred family tradition of planning and preparing elaborate birthday dinners for her parents and both older siblings.

Two weeks before each birthday, she would mail handmade invitations announcing the celebration dinner. Her mother would take her to the gourmet grocery store, and they would shop for ingredients for the menu that she had thoughtfully planned.

When the big day would arrive, she would set the table with the special-occasion china, including fresh flowers cut from the garden and beautifully inscribed name cards, always seating the guest of honor at the head of the table. As for the dinners themselves, they were nothing short of culinary masterpieces. Four times a year, she created a very memorable night for the family.

Over the next ten years, Elise's driving focus was learning the food business. She subscribed to dozens of industry magazines and worked every position imaginable from dingy diners to white-glove service catering companies. When she wasn't working, reading, or watching culinary shows, she would experiment, creating new dishes for her friends and family. After high school, she attended a renowned culinary institution, where she graduated with high honors.

Elise was a talented, passionate, hard worker. She was determined that one day she'd own her own business. A few days after her twenty-fifth birthday, she found the perfect place for sale. Between the money she had earned and prudently saved over the years and a loan from her parents, her lifetime dream was about to become a reality. After a month of cleaning and reorganizing, *Elise's Café and Catering* was ready to open for business.

The day before the official opening, filled with a mix of anxiety, excitement, and pride, she got in touch with her favorite instructor from her culinary school, Ms. Cody. Elise wanted to share her big news and to ask an important question.

"Ms. Cody, if you were to give me one piece of advice before I embark on this journey, what would it be?"

Ms. Cody paused, breathed a heavy sigh, and said, "Get into a different line of work."

Urban Legend? Perhaps.

However, if you are smiling, it's because you can relate to the message. Our industry has a well-earned reputation for being long on hours and short on profit. If this is your reality, starting or growing a corporate drop-off catering division can be your road to riches.

TIP:

It's still about building relationships.

Reality Catering

"Poor Me"

POOR ME

This was a painful, but necessary lesson.

One random Friday in July at the end of the day, I received a call from Sara, a regular customer. She wanted to discuss a catered event for the week after Labor Day. It was a lot of business: breakfast and lunch was needed Monday thru Friday for fifty people.

When she called, "Poor Me" was feeling a little cranky. We had just made it through a very hectic, understaffed week. My mind felt like mush. I just wanted to go home. She asked if I could give her a proposal the following Monday morning.

I wanted to scream (but didn't); "She has to wait until 4:00pm on Friday to spring this on me?" She said something about "being sorry it was such short notice, but she had a meeting scheduled with her boss Monday at 11am when they would review the proposal together, blah, blah, blah."

Don't get me wrong. It was a big job and I wanted the business. We had done a similar event for her six months prior, and it went well. She even mentioned her boss had been very pleased. But, c'mon. The week after Labor Day was six weeks away. We would need a half-hour to discuss the specifics, and it would take me about an hour to put a detailed proposal together.

Did I mention it was late in the day on a Friday in July? I was tired and all I wanted to do was go home. It is important to note that Poor Me (PM) had no specific plans that weekend. It wasn't like I had a plane to catch.

PM: "Sara, can we discuss this first thing Monday morning?"

Please note: This was a terrible idea...way too many things can intervene to prevent a proposal getting in her hands Monday morning. A few that come to mind are these (all of which have happened):

- Someone calls in sick and your morning routine is altered.
- You have a problem with your e-mail.
- Sara has an issue and can't talk as scheduled.
- You have car problems.
- The board of health shows up. (Oh, what joy their visits can be.)
- The power goes down, no phones, no computers = no proposal.
- Your produce vendor calls to say his truck broke down and your large,

important, time-sensitive delivery needed by 9am at the latest will be there by noon, hopefully.

SARA: "We can't do it now?"

PM: "I'm so sorry. Our computers are down, (lie #1) and, I'm about to leave for the airport for a friend's wedding in Chicago." (lie #2) The truth is I was going to Chicago for a friend's wedding - the following weekend.

SARA: "OK, I get in at 9am Monday."

PM: "Can I call you then?"

SARA: "Will that be enough time for my 11am meeting?"

PM: "No problem. That will be P L E N T Y of time."

SARA: " I'll let my boss know. Have fun in Chicago."

PM: "Thanks Sara." ("Yes!...I am SO out of here" I think to myself.)

Later That Evening

PM: In a more relaxed state, I reflect on the phone call with conflicting thoughts. "Breakfast and lunch for fifty people for five days...that's a lot of dough. When I took the call — instead of banging on my highchair, maybe I should have taken a breath, had a discussion, and e-mailed a proposal. I would still be home now – I mean in Chicago."

PM: Saturday: Going about my usual Saturday errands/business, I find my thoughts floating back to the situation. I think, "It'll be fine. Sara and I have a good working relationship. As long as I get her the proposal before her meeting, everything will work out. I should plan to go in early on Monday." I also worry about the embarrassment of bumping into her over the weekend. What the hell would I say? A snowstorm cancelled my flight... in July?

PM: Sunday: I acknowledge that whatever was so important about getting out of the office Friday feels like a very distant memory. I have to remember to handle these situations differently next time. It's not worth it. It's been nagging at me all weekend.

Monday Morning

PM: 8:00am - I leave Sara a voice mail, "Hi, Sara. I know you won't be in for another hour. Please call me as soon as you get settled in, so I can get you the proposal."

PM: 9:30am - I leave another, slightly panicked voice mail, "Hi, Sara. I was just checking to see if you are in yet. PLEASE call me ASAP. I know your meeting is in an hour and a half."

PM: 10:15am - Sensing doom, I leave one last message, "Hi, Sara. Maybe I misunderstood you. I thought we needed to speak first thing this morning. Please call me.

Monday Afternoon

SARA: 1:30pm - (leaves a voice mail) "Hi, I've had a crazy morning and am just getting your messages. After we spoke on Friday, my boss moved our meeting to 10:00am. He said I better call someone else as backup, in case I couldn't get your proposal in time. The morning traffic was a nightmare and I *just* made it to the meeting. So, because the timing got messed up, we are going with the other caterer. I'm sorry. There is another event in the spring, which I'll call you for. I hope you had fun in Chicago."

OUCH.

REALLY, REALLY IMPORTANT

This is what I took away from this "customer service growth opportunity":

When a customer calls, and makes any of these statements:

- "I'd like to place an order."
- "I'd like to get some information about your catering services."
- "I'd like to get a proposal."

This is code for:

"I WANT TO GIVE YOU MONEY."

When you get these calls, envision the customer literally extending their hand with a check made out to your business. Anytime you feel you have something more important to do, you are putting your hand up to stop them and saying, "I don't want your money now. Perhaps later, but this particular moment is not convenient for me. I have something more important to do."

PS. We did cater the spring event for Sara.

Needless to say, she received the proposal with plenty of time to spare.

TIP:

Document Everything!

TRIAL & ERROR CATERING

PART I

SITUATION
Defining "assorted" sandwiches.

Customers often ordered "20 assorted sandwiches"

WHAT WE THOUGHT THEN
Assorted means *assorted*. The sandwich maker will produce an appropriate variety.

WHAT WE KNOW NOW
If Carl Carnivore is the sandwich maker, "20 assorted" might include 1 vegetarian sandwich (too few). If Valerie Vegetarian is the sandwich maker, "20 assorted" might include 10 vegetarian sandwiches (too many).

LESSON LEARNED
Consider "assorted" a recipe term that requires definition and documentation.

The assortment should be consistent regardless of who the sandwich maker is.

Example: 20 Assorted Sandwiches:

4 Turkey
4 Chicken Salad
4 Vegetarian
3 Tuna Salad
3 Roast Beef
2 Ham

> *"People like consistency. Whether it's a store or a restaurant, they want to come in and see what you are famous for."*
>
> *Millard Drexler*
> *Chairman, CEO, J.Crew*

SITUATION
Determining how many sandwiches to include on orders.

WHAT WE DID THEN
For years, we included "1 extra sandwiches for every 10 ordered." (Example: sandwich order for 10 would receive 11, and an order for 20 would get 22).

WHAT WE DO NOW
Include 1 sandwich per person.

LESSON LEARNED
Our sandwiches are amply sized to begin with. It's more likely that someone would eat only half a sandwich as opposed to 1 ½. We were providing WAY too much food and not charging for it. (At the time, we were giving away 50-100 sandwiches per week...for nothing...OUCH!)

"In the 1960s, you could eat anything you wanted, and of course, people were smoking cigarettes and all kinds of things, and there was no talk about fat and anything like that, and butter and cream were rife. Those were lovely days for gastronomy, I must say."

Julia Child

SITUATION
Creating a product line.

WHAT WE DID THEN
Ordered what "we" liked. Whether it is beverages, bread, whole fruit, or muffin batter, people have a tendency to order in sync with their personal tastes. For example, if I don't like bananas or bran muffins, I am less inclined to include them in our product lines.

WHAT WE DO NOW
When we create an inventory list / order form, the rule is that 20% of the product line has to be items we would never purchase for our own consumption (because plenty of our customers do like bananas). In fact, according to the Department of Agriculture, bananas are Americans' most popular fruit.

LESSON LEARNED
Never assume that your personal preferences apply to the majority of your customers. When you are creating an inventory list / order form, ask your vendor representatives what their best-selling items are.

"Perfection is the enemy of profitability"

— *Mark Cuban*
The Shark Tank

SITUATION
Excessive variety/size of product lines.

WHAT WE THOUGHT THEN
"From soda to salad dressing to potato chips, the more choices the better. Doesn't everyone need Coke, Diet Coke, Caffeine-Free Diet Coke, Cherry Coke, Old Coke, New Coke, and In-between Coke" (not to mention an entire line of Pepsi products)?

WHAT WE KNOW NOW
Less can be more.

LESSON LEARNED
Information gathered from our customers and our account representative will determine the most popular varieties/flavors. Simplifying our product lines makes ordering easier, managing inventory more efficient, and the bottom line more profitable.

> *"It's always too soon to quit."*
>
> **Norman Vincent Peale**
> *Author, "The Power of Positive Thinking"*

SITUATION
In the early years, most of the items on our catering menu were priced and portioned by the platter size.

For example: <u>Vegetable Crudité:</u>

Small: serves 10-15 @ $45
Medium: serves 16-25 @ $75
Large: serves 26-35 @ $110

WHAT WE THOUGHT THEN
"This is how all other caterers seem to do it. It must be correct."

WHAT WE KNOW NOW
We realized that most of the platters were ordered for the next size down. For example, for 30 people, a customer would usually order the "medium," figuring "25 servings should be enough."

LESSON LEARNED
We experimented charging per person for everything (for example a customer could order vegetable crudité for 27 people at $3.50). Not only was portion control more accurate, the invoice total per person increased a few percentage points.

> "A brand for a company is like a reputation for a person. You earn reputation by trying to do hard things well."
>
> *Jeff Bezos*
> *Founder, Amazon.com*

SITUATION
Determining appropriate amounts of paper products for catering orders.

WHAT WE DID THEN
For years, we included 1½ pieces of paper products and plastic ware per person. (Example: sandwiches, tossed salad, and beverages for 20 people = 30 plates, 30 salad bowls, 30 forks, 30 knives, 30 napkins, and 30 cups).

WHAT WE DO NOW
We have reduced the quantity to between 1 and 1¼ pieces per person, depending on the item.

LESSON LEARNED
The difference between 1-1¼ and 1½ pieces of paper products may seem negligible. In fact, it resulted in tens of thousands of dollars savings per year. Eventually, we created written specs for "what gets what" for paper products for all orders. It maximizes profit margin and creates consistency.

"You can observe a lot just by watching."

Yogi Berra
Former Professional
Baseball Player

SITUATION
Catering deliveries being set up properly for our clients.

WHAT WE THOUGHT THEN
Since new delivery staff members are trained by veteran delivery staff, orders should be getting set up properly.

WHAT WE KNOW NOW
Our continental breakfasts come with hot cups, cold cups, plates, bowls, drip plates, napkins, forks, knives, butter, cream cheese, jam, stirrers, milkers, creamers, sugar, Splenda, spreaders, and serving utensils. When we set up a standing breakfast order for 50 people every Monday morning, it should look the same, week in and week out, regardless of who is setting it up. Without a diagram/manual, set-up will vary according to the person delivering meals that day. Remember this formula:

CONSISTENCY = REPEAT BUSINESS.

LESSON LEARNED
This is a perfect example of why a custom set-up manual for your catering division is a key component in achieving maximum success. It is the only way to ensure that nothing is missing and everything is arranged on the table exactly how you want it.

"Perhaps more than any other, the food industry is very sensitive to consumer demand."

Michael Pollan
Author

TIP:

Expect the unexpected.

REALITY CATERING

"HURRICANE BETH"

HURRICANE BETH

Beth was a good customer. She placed large orders for a law firm that had deep pockets. But she was tough and very particular. She wasn't shy about voicing her displeasure when something was not right.

For example, if we delivered her 7am Monday breakfast at 6:50am, she wouldn't think twice to call and ask why, "It was delivered so early?" Then, the following week she'd call at 7:05am demanding to know why, "breakfast isn't set up yet?" I think there are people in the world who are more comfortable complaining all the time. Beth was one of those people.

Truth be told, I was terrified of her.

One day it struck me that if she was not satisfied with our services, she would not continue to order. I decided to accept that she will usually find something to grumble about – and try to take it in stride. As long as we don't really screw something up, we should be ok.

One Thursday afternoon Beth called wanting to add tea to her 100-person breakfast for the next morning. "No problem," I said as I was looking up her order.

But there was a problem. I didn't have an order for her.

"I apologize, Beth. Can I call you back in a few minutes?"(I left out the part that I couldn't find her order).

After some investigation, hand wringing, and prayer, I figured it out. We had misdated the order for the FOLLOWING Friday. When I called back, I didn't mention that if she had not called to add tea that the only thing that would have arrived the next morning at 7am would have been Hurricane Beth – and it would have been a category 5 – for good reason.

I took the experience as a sign that a greater force had my back that day. But it was a one-time gift. To prevent it from happening again with a less fortunate outcome, we needed a better system. So, we implemented a second layer of cross-referencing for all of the next day's orders. And it's a good thing we did. Because it did occur again – more than once – but we always caught it.

So when something like this occurs, take it as a blessing and an opportunity to fix the flaw. And do it NOW. If you don't, you might not be so lucky the next time. And there will be a next time.

When building a new business, or sustaining its long-term success, it is imperative to continuously be contemplating and implementing methods of improving your internal systems. In fact, sometimes the longer you have been in business, the greater the need is to take a look around and assess what changes can be made for even smoother operations.

Lessons Learned From our Misstakes

TRIAL & ERROR CATERING

PART II

SITUATION
Same-day catering orders threw a wrench into daily operations.

WHAT WE DID THEN
Took the order(s)...whatever it was...and did our best to produce and deliver it (despite the mayhem it would occasionally cause.)

WHAT WE DO NOW
We offer a same-day menu (assorted sandwiches, salad of the day, drinks, desserts, and chips). When a customer calls at 10 a.m. and asks for lasagna, we say, "We can put together a great sandwich lunch."

LESSON LEARNED
As the catering business grows, requests for same-day orders increase, despite a "24-hour notice for delivery is required" policy. If a recurring situation is causing a strain on the operation, put your heads together and figure out a solution. Eliminate recurring frustration.

"Simplification is one of the most difficult things to do."

**Jonathan Ive
Senior Vice-President
Apple, Inc.**

SITUATION
One person, (the "expediter") was responsible for checking and verifying the accuracy of all out-going catering orders.

WHAT WE THOUGHT THEN
If one person is dedicated to checking out all orders, it should virtually eliminate mistakes.

WHAT WE KNOW NOW
As the business grows, opportunities for errors increase. It becomes increasingly difficult for one person to cross-check everything. There are simply too many details that can be overlooked.

LESSON LEARNED
For this system to work to maximum efficiency, orders need to be verified twice. The expediter was the first checkpoint. Each driver became the second and final checkpoint. When a driver was no longer able to shift responsibility for an imperfect order by claiming, "The expediter said I was all set," they had to take more ownership of their deliveries.

"The only thing I like better than talking about Food is eating."

John Walters
Musician

SITUATION
Hiring staff.

WHAT WE DID THEN
Talked with/interviewed potential employees once, (sometimes very briefly) and if all appeared good, we signed 'em up!

WHAT WE DO NOW
Bad hires cost time and money. No one is hired until we meet with them twice, (which is a good weeding-out process because half of potential hires don't show up for a second interview). Additionally, we speak with one or two past work references.

LESSON LEARNED
A job interview is similar to a first date. Everyone is on their best behavior, presenting themselves in the most positive light. When we hire an hourly employee we say, "We'll sit down again after two weeks and decide if this feels like a good fit on both ends."

> *"The five steps in teaching an employee new skills are preparation, explanation, showing, observation and supervision."*
>
> *Bruce Barton*
> *Congressman / Author*

Situation
Communicating with staff.

What We Did Then
When there was pertinent information or a new company policy to communicate, we either talked to staff individually or put memos in their paycheck envelopes.

What We Do Now
As our staff grew, it became much more efficient to schedule meetings. We keep a running list in the office titled: "Issues to be Discussed at Next Staff Meeting." When we get to #10 on the list, we schedule a meeting (approximately every other month).

Lesson Learned
Staff meetings are an opportunity to share information and experiences, ask questions, make suggestions, air grievances, and fix glitches. They can also be a morale booster for your employees.

> *"The single biggest problem in communication is the illusion that it has taken place."*
>
> ***George Bernard Shaw***
> ***Co-founder, London School of Economics / Playwright***

SITUATION
Hiring delivery drivers.

WHAT WE ASSUMED THEN
"Anyone applying for a driving position knows that they need a valid driver's license and a relatively good driving record."

WHAT WE KNOW NOW
Never Assume.

LESSON LEARNED
Anyone applying for a driving position must provide a copy of his or her license *and* driving record (which is available through the registry of motor vehicles).

> *"Never assume the obvious is true."*
>
> ***William Safire***
> ***Political Columnist,***
> ***New York Times***

SITUATION
A problem with an order was discovered at a customer's office.

WHAT WE DID THEN
Instructed the delivery person to call <u>our</u> office for trouble-shooting instructions.

WHAT WE DO NOW
Empower the delivery staff to problem-solve on their own when possible. Examples: if an order is missing salad dressing and they can buy some from the cafeteria in the building or a convenience store across the street, they do it (and always get a receipt for reimbursement).

LESSON LEARNED
If we are hiring properly, delivery staff will have the wherewithal to problem-solve some issues independently.

> *"Whatever words we utter should be chosen with care for people will hear them and be influenced by them for good or ill."*
>
> *Buddha*

SITUATION
Our delivery staff—the face(s) of our operation—was inconsistent.

WHAT WE THOUGHT THEN
"The delivery staff is well trained. They know how we want things done and the image we want to project. They will adhere to our guidelines and policies."

WHAT WE KNOW NOW
Despite our best efforts, our employees occasionally disappoint us. For example, at times you may have different definitions of "in uniform," "complete set-up," or "a clean van."

LESSON LEARNED
Your delivery personnel see your customers more than anyone else in your operation. The work they do needs to be spot-checked regularly. Their appearance and how they interact with your customers is how your business is perceived.

<u>Remember</u>: Perception = Reality.

> *"The best way to predict the future is to create it."*
>
> *Peter Drucker*
> *Management Consultant*

SITUATION
Replenishing backup paper goods.

WHAT WE THOUGHT THEN
"When a driver is setting up an order and discovers missing paper goods or serving utensils, the backup supply in every vehicle solves the problem. And then when that person returns from deliveries, it is their responsibility to replenish what they took."

WHAT WE KNOW NOW
This is one of those tasks that fall through the cracks. By the time the driver has returned, they may be preoccupied with equipment to unload, signed invoices to file, and their empty stomach to fill. Inevitably, some people remember to replenish, and others forget.

LESSON LEARNED
When tasks need to be done intermittently, assign one person.

Example: Every Friday afternoon, "Luke" is responsible for replenishing all backup paper goods in all vehicles.

" I had a brief experience in the food industry. I was a bus boy in a Mexican restaurant in Arizona, scraping re-fried beans off people's plates. It teaches you a bit of humility and the importance of a good deodorant."

Wentworth Miller
Actor / Screenwriter

TIP:

Don't try to be all things to all people.

REALITY CATERING

"LUNCH FOR (GULP) 500 PEOPLE"

LUNCH FOR 500 PEOPLE

One day I got a call from a woman, Mary, who wanted us to cater a luncheon for 500 people at the State House in Boston. I had been in business for about three years and was excited and nervous about this opportunity. It would definitely be the biggest job I had catered thus far. It was a high-profile event that could lead to more business, but there was a catch.

Our initial conversation went something like this:

Mary: "Hi, a colleague recommended your company to me. I need to organize a lunch next week for at least 500 people. Can you handle that size group?"

Me: "Absolutely," I replied, hoping my tone didn't betray the fear that had gripped every bone in my body.

So we began discussing the specifics – the day, place, time, budget, and menu. Then I asked, "When can you confirm the final number of people?"

Mary: "Well that's the tricky part. I won't know that for sure until the lunch actually gets going."

Me: "Um...ahh...ok...I'm sorry, could you elaborate on that?"

Mary: "These lunches at The State House can be, well, unpredictable. We never know for certain how many people are going to show up. What I usually do is order and pay for 500, and about a half-hour into the lunch, I let you know if we will need more food."

Me: "Umm...ok...could you give me a sense of how many more people you might need food for?"

Mary: "Anywhere from fifty to two-hundred."

Me: "OK, getting you more food isn't a problem. I can have my staff on stand-by, but if you end up needing a couple hundred more sandwiches, it's gonna take some time to produce and deliver them."

At this point I sensed that Mary was getting bored with our conversation. She gave a quick sigh and said, "I have been doing these lunches forever. They are a thorn in my side, and honestly, I'm not overly concerned about the details. I just want to get these savages (*her word*) fed, and move them along to their next event. The caterer that I usually order from gets whatever additional foods are needed over here pretty quickly. I don't know how they do it, and quite frankly, I don't care. I realize it'll take more than five minutes, but it can't take a half-hour. We may not even need any extra at all. But if it's something you'd rather not deal with, I understand completely."

She was a woman who knew what she wanted, and didn't mince words expressing it.

Me: "We definitely want to cater this lunch for you, Mary."

Mary: "Good, I have to run. Let's talk at the end of the week."

Before I could say goodbye, she hung up.

The next few days were spent working and worrying. How were we going to pull this off? It wasn't so much the number of people that concerned me, but rather the "I'll let you know half-way through lunch if we need a couple of hundred more sandwiches" part that was keeping me up at night.

There were three issues I needed to figure out.

First- how much backup/extra sandwich prep would we have on hand? (Sliced meats, cheeses, tuna and chicken salads, bread, condiments.) I decided on splitting her estimate and adding some. We would prep for an additional one hundred and fifty.

Second – how much staff was required if additional sandwiches were needed? We would be in the middle of the lunch rush – not exactly an ideal time to pull people off the floor. I decided to pad my lunch crew with extra staff who would be available to bang out up to two hundred sandwiches…quickly.

Third- how much personnel was needed to deliver and set-up round #1, and potentially round #2, to the State House? I contacted a temporary staffing agency and arranged for four servers to arrive at the restaurant a couple of hours before lunch was scheduled to begin.

Mary called as promised thirty minutes into the luncheon, needing food for "about a hundred more people" (= ten platters of sandwiches). I instructed two of the servers to high tail it back to the restaurant, which luckily was just around the corner. By the time they arrived, two of the ten platters were done.

Anxious to return to The State House, one of the servers, with more than a hint of panic in his voice asked,

"How long's it gonna be?"

"In fifteen minutes, we'll be done," a sandwich maker, responded. "Take these for now," handing off the two trays (= 20 sandwiches.)

"This it?" the server cried out, followed by the line that to this day, brings a smile to my face…"This like feedin' a tic-tac to a whale!"

There is nothing like a good, hearty group laugh to ease the tension of the moment.

This experience is a good example of an appropriate time to "go for it," and hopefully take your catering business to the next level. I felt I had enough experience with this type of lunch to go beyond my comfort zone and pull it off. Granted, there were new challenges to get through, but all in all, it was a success. It gave me confidence to take on more jobs this size.

Trial & Error Catering

Part III

SITUATION
For years, we ran a promotion: *"Get a Free Bag Lunch with Your Online Lunch Order."* (It was wildly popular.)

WHAT WE THOUGHT THEN
"We have been running this same promotion forever. Our customers must be tired of it. It's time to make a change." *(We did.)*

WHAT WE KNOW NOW
We have no idea what our customers are thinking unless we hear directly from them. They may not want a change. *(They didn't.)*

LESSON LEARNED
If we are considering a decision that will effect our customers, we need to talk to and/or survey them before we do anything. If it's not broken, don't fix it. *(We went back to the Free Bag Lunch promotion.)*

> *"It's been a founding principle of our company to listen to the customers, and not guess what they want."*
>
> **Montgomery Kersten**
> **"Angel" Investor**

SITUATION
Serving/presenting hot food.

WHAT WE DID THEN
Used disposable steam pans.

WHAT WE DO NOW
Offer the option of wire-frame chafing dishes.

LESSON LEARNED
Wire-frame chafers are an effective option for serving hot food. They are more manageable and time-efficient than hard chafers and keep food hot just as well. Additionally, we are able to add a set-up charge when our clients request them.

> *"Food is our common ground, a universal experience."*
>
> *James Beard*
> *"Dean of American Cookery"*

SITUATION

An unhappy customer reported, "Your delivery person was 30 minutes late and didn't even bother to call me!"

WHAT WE DID THEN

Gave the delivery driver an earful for "being 30 minutes late and not calling the customer." (The driver said, "I was like 10 minutes late, and I *did* call!")

WHAT WE DO NOW

Calmly ask delivery drivers for their side of the story.

LESSON LEARNED

When two people have different versions of the same event, ***the truth often lies somewhere in the middle***. Don't respond until you collect all pertinent information and determine what you feel actually happened. (The fact-finding mission revealed that the driver was 15 minutes late and had left a voice mail).

> *"Your most unhappy customer is your greatest source of learning."*
>
> *Bill Gates*
> *Former CEO, Microsoft /*
> *Philanthropist*

SITUATION
We had limited communication with our bigger corporate accounts.

WHAT WE THOUGHT THEN
"No news is good news. They wouldn't have us catering these big standing orders if they weren't happy."

WHAT WE KNOW NOW
All clients want to feel appreciated. Staying in regular contact and proactively addressing issues as they arise is our responsibility (especially with bigger accounts).

LESSON LEARNED
NEVER take our regular accounts, the lifeblood of our business, for granted. Schedule face-to-face "Caterer Evaluation" meetings two or three times a year.

" I have always believed you cannot run a successful enterprise from behind a desk."

*Lou Gerstner
Former CEO, IBM*

SITUATION
Due to significant service issues with our coffee supplier, we changed vendors.

WHAT WE THOUGHT THEN
"We still use a French Roast coffee bean. Our customers probably won't even know the difference."

WHAT WE KNOW NOW
Our customers notice everything: good, bad, and in-between.

LESSON LEARNED
If you're going to change a product that you sell lots of (for example, coffee), proceed with caution. Get input from your most important tasters—your customers. Once you've made a change, the majority of unhappy customers won't tell you verbally; they'll voice their dissatisfaction by taking their business elsewhere.

"Don't let the mistakes and disappointments of the past control and direct your future."

Zig Ziglar
Motivational Speaker

SITUATION
Potential clients would ask us to "cater a breakfast for 4 people" or "deliver a hot lunch for $8 per person," and we would say or imply, "No."

WHAT WE SAID THEN
"I'm sorry, no, we don't deliver breakfast for fewer than 7 people," or, "I'm sorry, that is not a reasonable budget for a hot lunch."

WHAT WE SAY NOW
Tell them what we CAN do.

LESSON LEARNED
We don't ever have to say "NO" to our customers.
For example:
"Our minimum for breakfast delivery is for 7. Would it be possible to round up a few more people from your office? Or, perhaps you could surprise a few people in the morning with breakfast!?"
OR...
"We have delicious sandwiches and salads. We could put together a nice combination of both within your budget. Can I describe an example for you?"
OR...
"The hot entrees are very popular. They are available in the $12-$15 per person price range."

"We see our customers as invited guests to a party, and we are the hosts. It's our job every day to make every important aspect of the customer experience a little bit better."

Jeff Bezos
Founder, Amazon.com

SITUATION
We had delays getting our delivery vehicles into the bays of the busy office buildings (due to multiple vendors making deliveries around the same time).

WHAT WE DID THEN
Waited and worried.

WHAT WE DO NOW
Build relationships with the people running the bays by "thanking/bribing" them with a sandwich or cookie; it is worth its weight in gold.

LESSON LEARNED
Food is a strong bartering chip. Take advantage of it. (Remember, your cost is only 1/3 the price you charge.)

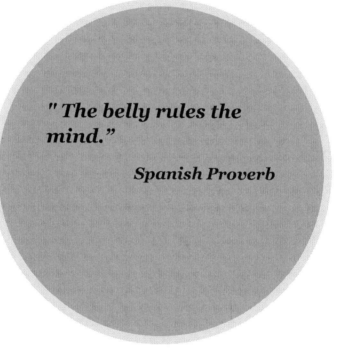

" The belly rules the mind."

Spanish Proverb

SITUATION
Missing Equipment: we were continuously purchasing new airpots, Cambros, warming bags, and carts to replace the ones that had vanished from our clients' offices.

WHAT WE THOUGHT THEN
"It's the cost of doing business."

WHAT WE KNOW NOW
Equipment is very expensive to replace. Our clients need to assume responsibility for any hardware we provide them.

LESSON LEARNED
It was amazing how we suddenly got everything back when we added this to the menu/website: "Client is responsible for the cost of any unrecoverable equipment."

"Seeing a catering truck feels like home."

Dakota Johnson
Actress

TIP:

Before launching a new marketing campaign, get a couple of objective opinions.

REALITY CATERING

"DOING THE MATH"

DOING THE MATH

I had a guy working for me who was in charge of assembling set-ups. (This was before I created a set-up manual). One day I asked him, "When you're doing a lunch set-up, how do you decide how many plates to include?"

His response was, "Two per person. I figure some people may need a second one, maybe more people will show up — we don't want to run out of plates."

"Hmmm," I thought, "I should take a closer look at this."

- We were delivering 150 lunches per week, for an average of 15 people per order = 2,250 people served a week.
- 2,250 @ 2 plates per person = 4,500 plates per week
- At a cost of .09¢ per plate = $405 per week

After some debate we decided to provide 1¼ plates per person.

- So, instead of 4,500 plates per week, it was now 2,815 (1,685 less plates) @ .09 = $150 per week
- $150 x 50 weeks = $7,500

So, faster than you can say, "That should cover

the cost of a nice weeklong vacation – for 2," we added $7,500 to the bottom line by adjusting the quantity of **ONE ITEM.**

Just think of all the additional adjustments that could be made — napkins, forks, knives, bowls, beverage cups, mayo/mustard, etc.

(PS. Ten years later, 1¼ plates per person was working just fine.)

Tip:

"If you are patient in a moment of frustration, you will escape 100 days of sorrow."

Lessons Learned From our Misstakes

TRIAL & ERROR CATERING

PART IV

SITUATION
A decision about food costs

WHAT WE THOUGHT THEN
"To realize a maximum profit margin, all expenses, especially food, should be as minimal as possible."

WHAT WE KNOW NOW
We do <u>not</u> cut corners when it comes to our food. We'd rather charge more for a great product.

LESSON LEARNED
Food is our product. To generate repeat business over a long period of time, we need to build a reputation of providing generous portions of delicious food.

> *"I judge a restaurant by the bread and by the coffee."*
>
> ***Burt Lancaster***
> ***Actor***

Situation
While delivering lunch to a company in a high-rise, we were asked, "What catering company are you from? Your vans are in front of the building every day, but all I can see from the 17th floor is the white roof."

What We Did Then
Told them the name of our company.

What We Do Now
Put our website and phone number on the ROOF of the delivery vehicles.

Lesson Learned
Our delivery trucks are a great opportunity for marketing and advertising. A lot of people see them every day. Maximize visibility.

" Everyone who's ever taken a shower has an idea. It's the person who gets out of the shower, dries off and does something about it that makes a difference."

Nolan Bushnell
Founder, Atari, Inc.

SITUATION
Getting new business from existing clients.

WHAT WE THOUGHT THEN
"If we're doing a good job, the companies we deliver to will give us as much catering business as they have."

WHAT WE KNOW NOW
The companies we deliver to, especially the bigger ones, oftentimes order from multiple catering companies. Some departments operate autonomously and don't always share information, so don't expect those contacts to say, "If you are looking for a new catering company, I order from a great one."

LESSON LEARNED
Satisfied clients can be a powerful source of new business. Try asking this... "Amanda, thank you for your loyal business. We really appreciate it. Our staff sees lots of different caterers delivering to your company. Would you be able to help schedule a day when we could come in and provide a complimentary tasting for all the administrators who have not ordered from us? We are hoping for an opportunity to expand our customer base within your company."

"Even if you are on the right track, you will get run over if you just sit there."

Will Rogers
Actor / Social Commentator

Situation
Working with companies such as Foodlers, Seamless, and Grubhub.

What We Thought Then
"Working with web-based food delivery companies is a hassle that cuts into our profits. We want nothing to do with them."

What We Know Now
Working with web-based food delivery companies is a hassle that cuts into our profits. However, our competitors use them, and it appears that these services are more than a passing fad. We reluctantly partner with them. Can these companies bring you business that you wouldn't get otherwise? Yes, but at a cost—and the costs vary. Some make the deliveries (which brings up another set of issues) and charge a higher commission. Some suggest that you charge higher prices when using them (to compensate for their cut), and others don't allow it. Some add their own delivery charge, while others apply a percentage-based gratuity. Keeping it all straight can be a job all unto itself.

Lesson Learned
If you work with any web-based food delivery companies, be sure you understand the financial arrangement. Negotiate terms that keep these orders in the black (= profitable). Confirm that the agreements are being followed. Remember, more things are negotiable than you may realize. Consider these types of companies as more of a vendor than a customer.

"Willingness to change is a strength, even if it means plunging part of the company into total confusion for a while."

Jack Welch
Former CEO, General Electric

Situation
A prospect called to say, "My boss asked me to get quotes from three caterers. We need breakfast and lunch for 25 people, all next week."

What We Said Then
"That will cost X amount per person. Please give us a call back if you would like to book with us."

What We Say Now
"We'd be happy to quote you a price. May we please start with your name, phone number, and email address?"

Lesson Learned
Always get contact information from prospective clients. A follow-up call could land you the job – or future business.

> *"Marketing is not an event, but a process...It has a beginning, a middle, but never an end. You improve it, perfect it, change it, even pause it. But you never stop it completely."*
>
> *Jay Conrad Levinson*
> *Author, "Guerilla Marketing"*

SITUATION
Negotiating better pricing from our vendors.

WHAT WE THOUGHT THEN
"Their prices are what they are. If we think we are paying too much, we need to find a different vendor."

WHAT WE KNOW NOW
LOTS of things are negotiable.

LESSON LEARNED
Do you ever get a call from a client or prospect requesting a price break? Do they sometimes get one? Are you ready for a very sophisticated tactic for negotiating better pricing? Here it is...
ASK.

"The food business is very tough, but there's also a lot of love and giving."

*Marcus Samuelsson
Restaurateur*

SITUATION
Tracking the prices that our vendors charge us.

WHAT WE THOUGHT THEN
We always get the best possible pricing from all our vendors.

WHAT WE KNOW NOW
A percentage point or two can be significant in our industry. While vendors' prices do increase occasionally (just as yours do), it's crucial to pay close attention to the money going out the door. Never assume the prices you are paying for products are rock bottom. (Are your menu prices rock bottom?)

LESSON LEARNED
Someone in your operation should be responsible for keeping a very close eye on your invoices. It's not unheard of for a vendor who wants your business to undercut the competition to get your account and then gradually increase prices over time. Some products, such as produce, fluctuate regularly depending on the time of year or market conditions. If you notice that your pricing is creeping up across the board, call your vendors about it immediately. If they don't have a good explanation, it probably won't arbitrarily happen again. Also, consider putting your business "out to bid" from time to time. And let the specific vendors know you are doing so. Keep 'em on their toes.

> *"Nothing focuses the mind better than the constant sight of a competitor who wants to wipe you off the map."*
>
> *Wayne Calloway*
> *Former CEO, Pepsi*

SITUATION
Maximizing what your vendors can do for you.

WHAT WE THOUGHT THEN
"Our vendors will proactively do everything possible to keep us satisfied customers."

WHAT WE KNOW NOW
Some vendors (such as Coke and Pepsi) have liberal latitude when it comes to providing expensive equipment for your operation. In theory, a 3-door Coke cooler is supplied exclusively to sell Coke products. In reality, if it's being used as additional refrigeration in your basement, some account representatives will look the other way to keep your business.

LESSON LEARNED
Having your vendors supply your operation with refrigeration units and new coffee machines/equipment oftentimes means simply asking for it.

"Fettuccini alfredo is macaroni and cheese for adults."

Mitch Hedberg
Stand-up Comedian

TIP:

Remember the big picture.

REALITY CATERING

"DIVIDE AND CONQUER"

DIVIDE & CONQUER

The following is a recreated script of an actual negotiation with Coca-Cola. (Note: Some names have been changed, to protect the innocent).

<u>Corporate Caterer (=CC)</u>: "Hi, Vinny (the account rep). I have been doing a thorough analysis of our larger volume vendors. Coke is one of them and I'd like to share some thoughts with you."

<u>Coke</u>: "Sure, go right ahead."

<u>CC</u>: "Great, thanks. First, let me say that Coke has done a good job for us. Ordering is easy, deliveries arrive as scheduled, office staff is professional, invoicing is efficient, and you personally have come thru for us when we've needed something in a pinch.

<u>Coke</u>: "Ok, so far so good!"

<u>CC</u>: I have been in contact with Nancy Richards from your distribution center. She researched our purchasing history. Over the last two-and-a-half years, our average order has been thirty-five cases a week. You will notice our volume has increased over the last six months.

<u>Coke</u>: "I have noticed."

CC: "Great. I've discovered that our price per case has increased from $8.20 to $8.85 over this time. Recently, through aggressive sales work, we've experienced growth in our corporate catering division. We see some real opportunity here, and are committed to focusing on this area of the business. As we grow, we will need more Coke product to sell.

Coke: "Ok, still so far so good!"

CC: "Based on our increased volume and our payment history, I am requesting a price reduction."

Coke: "Oh, not as good"

REALLY, REALLY IMPORTANT: *Have a target figure in mind for the new case price. In this discussion, it was the original $8.20 per case. ALWAYS have the vendor be the first to offer a revised price, as it could be lower than what you are seeking.*

Coke: "Would you forward me the numbers Nancy compiled?"

CC: "No problem. Thanks for taking a look."

This is an appropriate request. Do not expect an immediate response. Although with independent companies, it can happen.

Coke: "Give me a few days to go through them, and I'll give you a call."

CC: "Sounds good. Thanks again."

Don't be surprised if a few days pass and you haven't heard back. No matter how much business you do with them, lowering your pricing will not be tops on Vinny's to-do list. You may have to call him again. Don't be shy about doing so.

CC: (message) "Hi, Vinny. It's been almost a week since we spoke about our pricing situation. I'd appreciate you calling me today. Thank you."

Vinny calls back:

Coke: "What did you have in mind for a price adjustment?"

CC:" I would be more comfortable hearing your thoughts first."

Coke: "OK. I looked over the numbers Nancy compiled and spoke with my boss. How about if we drop your price to $8.50 a case?"

CC: "I appreciate your willingness to discuss this, Vinny. Thank you, because this is an important issue for us. And I don't want to hassle you about this in another six months. I was hoping you would come in a little more aggressively and we could agree on $8.00 a case."

Coke: "$8.00 a case? I can't do that. We would be losing money. I might be able to go to, say $8.35 or $8.40, but that's it."

CC: "Vinny, I realize you have numbers to meet. We all do. I am confident our commitment to corporate catering will generate more business, which should easily offset a slightly lower margin. In the spirit of the good working partnership we have, and hope will continue to have, we could see our way to pay $8.20 case, but no more."

Coke: "I'll have to talk to my boss and get back to you."

CC: "No problem, I understand. Can you please let me know by the end of the week?"

Two days later, Vinny calls.

Coke: "Ok. You've got a deal at $8.20 a case."

Over the course of one year, based on ordering 1,750 cases, the difference between $8.85 a case and $8.20 a case equals $1,137.50.

REALLY, REALLY IMPORTANT

Successfully negotiating a price reduction is great. But if in six months your invoices start creeping up again, the full savings will not be realized. Make this part of the negotiation conversation. Coke may say they cannot make a time commitment regarding pricing, because they cannot predict future market conditions.

If possible, you would like to know the adjustment will remain in place for a minimum of one year, preferably longer — and if you can get it in writing, even better.

Another angle to work is refrigeration. For example, Coke says, "Based on the current volume you are purchasing, $8.50 is as low as we can go." Or, "$8.85 is the case price for our top tier customers. We don't go any lower."

Most of the big beverage distributors will provide refrigeration units at no cost and will deliver them to you. This is <u>A BIG DEAL</u>. These units are expensive. Depending on the vendor, there are different options ranging from a single door slider to a 4-door mega unit. Your space and volume will be part of the equation, but experience has shown that the reps tend to be pretty flexible.

Granted, the intention of supplying these expensive units is to have them displayed in your restaurant, filled exclusively with their products. They are not meant for your lower level kitchen as a storage unit for produce. But even in this situation, a lot of reps will look the other way. So, if you could use additional, bigger, or newer units you might suggest to the vendor:

<u>CC</u>: "How about $8.50 a case and two additional refrigeration units?"

What if the Negotiation is not going so well?

You have options. Just as you are not the only corporate catering game in town, Coca-Cola isn't the only beverage distributor either. During negotiations, try to remain positive, professional, polite, and firm. In the end, you are dealing with living, breathing people. An attitude of "we are partners working together towards a resolution" gets you further in the end.

However, there is a time and place when you need to dig in a little deeper.

The example negotiation with Coke was relatively straightforward and easy. At no time did the caterer mention the dreaded "P" word

— Pepsi. But, let's say that the responses to the requests for (1) better pricing, (2) refrigeration, or (3) a combination of both are "No, no, and no."

SUGGESTION

CC: "I'm sorry that is Coke's position. [You intentionally do not say "your" position.] And although this is not the direction I wanted to go, I am going to have to explore my other options. I will be in touch."

Time to Contact Pepsi

- This will be a process.
- At times, it may feel frustrating.
- Hang in there.
- It will be worth it.

You may get bounced around a few times, and end up leaving a voice mail for the sales rep in charge of your area. From experience, it is possible that days will pass and you will not hear back from them. Although you cannot comprehend the concept of not receiving a call back immediately after leaving a message stating, *"We have been ordering regularly from* [insert competitors name], *and are considering making a change."* However, there are a lot of unmotivated people out there.

- So don't be surprised if you have to call again.
- Pepsi will probably want to set up a meeting. (They should come to you.)
- Let them know that you would like a written pricing package. To do this, you will need to tell them how much you are purchasing from Coke.

REALLY, REALLY IMPORTANT

Do not forget to discuss your refrigeration needs. Tell them what Coke is currently supplying you with. This is absolutely the time to decide if you need additional units and this information should be included in their presentation package.

You will use this information as a negotiation tool when you get back in contact with Coke

If You Tell Anyone You Read This Here, It Will Be Denied!

Amazingly, neither vendor appears to be that diligent about their refrigeration once it arrives at a destination. Experience has revealed that if a switch from one to the other does happen, sometimes the replaced vendor will never pick up their units. In this case, the only responsible step is to continue to use them so they do not breakdown due to lack of use. (wink, wink).

If you do make a change, do NOT call Coke and say, "we are switching to Pepsi so you can pick up your refrigeration." For starters, you want to see how it goes with Pepsi. It is not even necessary to tell Coke you're doing this. Just don't call to place an order. If they call you, tell them you are "all set at the moment." If after a few weeks, a rep from Coke puts two and two together and calls or shows up at your business, then say you are "trying this out", which you are.

If Pepsi does not meet your expectations, you could be back with Coke. So, it would make sense for them to leave the refrigeration, at least for the time being. If Pepsi does work out and you decide to stay with them, it will be Coke's responsibility to contact you and arrange for pick-up.

Back to the Negotiating Table

REALLY, REALLY IMPORTANT

Pepsi may ask, "What are you currently paying for your Coke products?"

Do not, Do not, DO NOT – UNDER ANY CIRCUMSTANCES, ANSWER THIS

QUESTION. (There might be a time to reveal this — later.)You can respond, politely but firmly, "That is not something I am going to discuss at this time." PERIOD.

You will need to tell them how much product you are purchasing.

This will affect the bid they present. But it can vary. For example, at 35 cases a week, a rep may quote you anywhere from $8 to $9 per case.

You are dealing with a rep who wants to brag to his boss that he landed a nice new account, and one that had been with Coke as an added feather in his cap. Without knowing how much you are currently paying, the rep may come in closer to $8 than $9. If Pepsi knows you are paying $8.85, perhaps they bid $8.50. If they know you are paying $8.25, perhaps they come in at $8.00. The point is that you want their best or close-to-best pricing right off the bat. This is how to get the price you want and perhaps do even better than you hoped.

What If You Are Not Satisfied With The Proposed Pricing?

Now is the time to let them know what you are paying and be prepared to back it up with recent invoices. All other terms being equal (coolers, payment terms, and delivery schedule), tell Pepsi the following:

"It's just not worth the hassle (and it is a hassle) of making such a big change to save only $0.35 a case." At this point you can add, "For this to make sense for us, we would need to pay (fill in the amount, such as $8.20) a case."

The ball is now back in their court.

Remember, this is possibly all in the spirit of negotiating a better deal with Coke. Granted, you may actually switch to Pepsi — time will tell. The rep will most likely say, "I'm going to have to check with my boss and get back to you."

When Pepsi proposes their final bid, have them put it in writing.

- **Time to Contact Coke**

CC: "Vinny, I hope we can hammer out an agreement that will allow us to do business together for a long time, but I need to have a plan B if we can't come to an agreement. Pepsi has been knocking on my door for years. A rep was here last week and they have an offer on the table for $8.25 a case. They have agreed to lock-in this case price for at least the next twelve months. And, they are offering two additional refrigeration units. Coke needs to at least meet, if not beat this offer. Can we make a deal?"

After the Negotiations

It is crucial to keep an eye on your invoices after striking a new deal and making sure pricing remains at the agreed upon amount. Just like spot-checking weights, your vendors know which of their customers keep a vigilant eye on invoices. Act promptly and appropriately if there is an issue.

TIP:

Begin sales campaigns in your own backyard.

TRIAL & ERROR CATERING

PART V

SITUATION
We were asked to cater "an authentic clambake (cooked under sand) on a beach for 200 people" (we'd never catered a clambake).

WHAT WE SAID THEN
"200 people! Absolutely! We'd love to!"

WHAT WE SAY NOW
"Authentic clambakes are not our area of expertise. We suggest you work with a caterer who specializes in them."

LESSON LEARNED
Don't try to be all things to all people. If you want to expand your menu offerings into unchartered waters, throw a "Work out the Kinks Party" for friends and family. (We ended up getting help with this event from a colleague who was experienced with clambakes. If we hadn't...hoo boy – it would NOT have gone well).

"Be a yardstick of quality. Some people aren't used to an environment where excellence is expected."

Steve Jobs
Co-founder, Apple

SITUATION
Our catering menu stated, "No Substitutions."

WHAT WE THOUGHT THEN
"Without this policy, customers would be making crazy substitution requests all the time. It would create mayhem in the kitchen."

WHAT WE KNOW NOW
Most people are reasonable, and substitutions are not a big deal. For the occasional rogue request to substitute shrimp cocktail for a salad, we give it to 'em and charge appropriately.

LESSON LEARNED
"No Substitutions" became "Substitutions – No Problem!" (a much more customer-friendly policy).

"Make your product easier to buy than your competition, or you will find customers buying from them, not you."

Mark Cuban
Owner, NBA's Dallas Mavericks

SITUATION
Paying attention to the almighty details.

WHAT WE THOUGHT THEN
Details, such as the coffee machine being cleaned regularly and delivery orders being set up properly are crucial toward our success. As long as we assign specific tasks to specific people, things should get done properly.

WHAT WE KNOW NOW
The coffee machine will be cleaned regularly and delivery orders will be set up properly as long as we assign specific tasks to specific people...*and have a system that confirms completion.*

LESSON LEARNED
Check. Confirm. Verify. Taste your coffee. Sample your food. Spot-check that set-ups are being done correctly. (Have you ever stopped by a client's office to look at the set-up? Try it... your client will love it, and it's a great opportunity to connect with them face to face.)

> *"I told the caterer I'd work for nothing if he'd teach me about catering. I lasted one week full-time. It was exhausting."*
>
> **Diane Mott Davidson**
> *Best-Selling Author*

SITUATION
Controlling your accounts receivable.

WHAT WE THOUGHT THEN
We provide catering services for reputable, well-run companies. We'll bill them for our services, and they'll pay us on time.

WHAT WE KNOW NOW
LOL. If only it were that easy. Once you start billing, you will always be owed money. As your business grows, your "past dues" will increase. It's VERY important to have an organized system for tracking every dollar that you are owed.

LESSON LEARNED
While most corporate accounts get billed once and pay on time, chasing money is a reality of any business. Someone in your operation needs to be responsible for regularly monitoring the money you're owed. When an account becomes past due, call and ask to speak to the accounts payable department. Set up a database with the contact of the person who handles your account.

Suggested opening dialogue:
"Hi (first name), this is Michael from The Corporate Caterer. I'd like to check on some open invoices that are showing in our system."

" The buck stops with the guy who writes the checks."

Rupert Murdoch
Founder, FOX News Corporation

SITUATION
Turning away business.

WHAT WE THOUGHT
Regardless of how busy we were, we NEVER turned away business. One way or another, we'd figure out how to get all the food ready and delivered on time.

WHAT WE KNOW NOW
Having more business than you can comfortably handle is a good problem, as long as you manage it correctly. Once in a while, despite pulling out all the stops (for example, having the entire kitchen crew making deliveries), we hit a ceiling. Accepting more orders for an 11:45 delivery is not always logistically possible.

LESSON LEARNED
Taking on business that you cannot handle properly makes no sense. If necessary, we say, "We are fully booked with deliveries until 12:30. We're happy to deliver lunch to you between 12:30 and 1:00 if that works. Or, you are welcome to pick it up as early as you'd like."

" If anything is good for pounding humility into you permanently, it's the restaurant business."

Anthony Bourdain, Chef

SITUATION
Responding to slower business months.

WHAT WE USED TO DO:
We struggled. In the early years, January, February, July, and August were always the slowest for the corporate catering business. Cutting back on labor can be tricky. Full-time employees did not (and in most cases, could not) survive on a part-time salary for 1/3 of the year. Yet, we couldn't keep a full-time staff when business would drop off by 20%.

WHAT WE DO NOW
All full-time staff members become involved in the sales process during the slow months. Delivery drivers drop off complimentary dessert trays and gather lists of building directories. Prep/kitchen personnel stuff envelopes for direct mail campaigns. Office workers make cold calls and prospect for new leads.

LESSON LEARNED
January, February, July, and August are great months to go after new business. If you make a sales plan and stick to it, before long, your revenue stream will be steadier than you ever imagined, and these months won't be so slow anymore!

"Leadership is solving problems. The day soldiers stop bringing you their problems is the day you have stopped leading them. They have either lost confidence that you can help or do not care. Either case is a failure of leadership"

Colin Powell
Former Secretary of State
Retired Four-Star General, US Army

TIP:

Customer service rule #1: Follow-up sooner, rather than later.

SUMMARY THOUGHTS AND SUGGESTIONS

(1) MENU

Create a separate corporate catering menu. Piggyback off your existing menu, focusing on food that will transport well. Continental breakfasts and sandwiches are two of the most commonly ordered items. Feature a signature specialty that will generate some buzz and differentiate you from competitors. Some examples include great coffee, beautiful sliced fruit platters, home roasted sandwich meats, freshly baked breads, locally sourced vegetables for salads, or "the best" chocolate chip cookies in town.

TIP: If you are composing a corporate catering menu for the first time, begin with a smaller one. As your business grows, so can your menu.

(2) PRICING

If you operate a restaurant, the pricing structure for your catering menu should be higher than the restaurant menu, across the board. Clients expect to pay more for the convenience and efficiency of delivery. Prices are customarily listed on a per-person or platter-size basis. Most items should be offered buffet style. As a rule, your overall food cost for corporate catering should be no more than 33% of your total costs.

TIP: Research your competitors pricing structure, and consider how you want to position yours, comparatively.

(3) POLICIES

Policies must be established for delivery area, delivery charges, hours of operation, minimum quantities, advance notice requirements, same-day orders, special requests, substitutions, cancellations, and payment terms. Despite your best efforts to have all orders placed a day in advance, you will get calls for same-day and last minute catering. In fact, as your business grows, so to will these requests. While they can throw a wrench into your best-laid plans, the revenue they can generate can be significant. Use the policies as a guideline, but be flexible when you can, especially for larger clients. People like it when you break policy for them; it makes them feel special.

TIP: Consider offering a more limited, prep-friendly menu when a customer calls at 10:30 a.m. to request a lunch delivery at noon.

4) PACKAGING

Arrange for three paper companies to present sample lines of their disposable service ware for catering. Options are plentiful for both styles and colors. Consider incorporating recyclable/reusable plastic ware when possible. In recent years, sustainable packaging has become a requirement for some companies who use caterers. If the plastic ware and paper products you provide are environmentally friendly, be sure to include this information on the menu and website.

TIP: Inform vendors that you are expanding your catering business, and ask them to present their most aggressive bottom-line pricing. Inform them that you are getting multiple bids.

(5) DELIVERY

Whether it is by vehicle, on foot, or a third-party delivery service, efficiently transporting on-time catering orders to your clients is as important as the food itself. Your delivery staff is most often the face(s) of your operation. Responsible, polite representatives, who make their customers feel that their delivery is the most important of the day, will help forge relationships that lead to repeat business.

TIP: In the inevitable event that something is missing from a set-up, all delivery vehicles should have backup paper products and serving utensils. Additionally, all representatives should be properly trained in trouble-shooting solutions for when problems arise.

(6) MARKETING

Successful marketing may consist of a combination of direct, social, in-house, paid, and word-of-mouth practices. An effective marketing program should include a coordinated, well-planned fusion of sales, service, packaging, and promotion, with the intention of interlinking all components to achieve your overall marketing goals. A well-executed marketing program will keep your business fresh in the minds of your customers.

TIP: Holding a tasting at a potential new client's office is one of the most effective means to acquire new business and to showcase your food. (Who says there's "No such thing as a Free lunch?)

(7) CONSISTENCY

Consistency means giving your customers what they want—every single time. When customers feel a connection to your food and service, they will be loyal to your business. If you have lofty sales goals for your catering division, the most important components are consistency (product), consistency (service), and consistency (customer experience).

TIP: Innovation and customization can and should be prevalent, as long as the same consistency principles apply.

(8) PROCEDURAL SYSTEMS

Systems and processes are the building blocks of a successful business. Every facet of your operation should be part of a system that can be managed and improved by applying correct principles. Ideally, this approach eliminates employee indiscretion and replaces it with detailed procedures, standards, and accountability and includes a method for measuring results.

TIP: Use specs, diagrams, and pictures to define "how-to" steps for everything. (Example: Turkey sandwich = 4 oz. sliced turkey, 2 tomato slices, 1 oz. slice Swiss cheese, and 1 lettuce leaf).

(9) DOCUMENTATION

Put everything in writing. Systems documentation is an organized, detailed, thorough strategy for all key routines, daily tasks, and backup plans. It needs to be readily accessible and understandable to all your employees.

TIP: Creating a detailed, documented "playbook" for your entire operation will increase the value and, probably, the selling price of your business.

(10) INFORMATION RESOURCES

Educate yourself about the industry. There is a wealth of information available to stay up-to-date on current trends and relevant news information. Read trade magazines, research information on the Internet, sign up for webinars, take classes, and stay connected with colleagues in the field.

TIP: Set aside the first thirty minutes of each morning to educate yourself. Embrace new technology. From a big picture perspective, this practice will do your business a great service.

TESTIMONIALS

"The Corporate Caterer's Leads Program WORKS! We've bought 12 Leads Lists in the past year. Now, instead of spending half their time cold calling, my sales reps are doing what they do best...selling!"

- S.G.
City Kitchen, Fort Worth, Texas

"As an instructor in a hospitality department of a local Junior College, I will refer your company to my students so they can use you as a resource when they start restaurants and food service operations in the future."

-Paul McKenna
Starship Catering, Chicago, Ill

"I would like to thank Michael for our recent coaching hour. I am an executive chef turned salesperson. Michael's strategies are helping. I would highly recommend his personal coaching to anyone. Bon Appetit!"

-Christine M. Todaro
Cozy Caterers, Providence, RI

"We've been in business for over 25 years. Michael's insight on how to grow our catering operations was extremely helpful. He mentioned things I've overlooked or didn't even consider... details that have made a big difference to our bottom line. Thank you!"

LaTanya Holland
Lefty's BBQ, Washington, DC

"Michael Rosman is professional and approachable. He has really taken the time to understand our goals as a business and I feel confident in the strategies he's helped us develop to achieve those goals. After only a few months, we've seen an increase in our corporate catering business. His patience and experience has been a true asset to my growth as a sales person. The investment we've made in The Corporate Caterer has already and will continue to, pay off. "

-Ruth Hedges
Sales Associate, Gance's Complete Catering
Binghamton, NY

"I've been struggling for a clear direction in my businesses. I've owned an off-premise catering company for over 10 years and just recently opened a new restaurant. Michael has helped me achieve clarity and supported me in making big decisions. With his expertise, he is really helping me build the foundation for my companies so I can grow them on the right path. His direction towards the results I desire are very to the point and compassionate.

Thank you Michael for your support and I am looking forward to continuing working together! "

-Marita Lynn
Marita Lynn Catering & RUNA Restaurant
Aberdeen, New Jersey

"We are in our 37th year of a restaurant AND catering service who specialize in drop-off catering throughout all of Chicago. If anything, after reviewing your materials, it has reaffirmed that we are on target with our approach to growth and our day-to-day retention of customers."

-Paul McKenna
Starship Catering, Chicago, Ill

"Michael, I love your site! It is really helpful for our catering company. The templates work perfectly. They are very useful in formatting an operation. Thanks and keep up with your wonderful work! "

-Marcelo Politi
Nove EventosSan Pueblo, Brazil

"The Corporate Caterers Leads Program is incredible. No more cold calling! They do all the "grunt work." The first Leads List we purchased generated over $20,000 in new catering business catering in less than 3 months!"

-M. Ricarte
Via Lago Café & Catering
Boston, MA

"Mike was down to earth and very knowledgeable about the business of corporate drop-off catering. It was an absolute pleasure to talk with someone who had experienced so many of the same things I am as my business expands. City Kitchen Catering will definitely be seeking his consultation in the future."

-Bob Orem
City Kitchen Catering
Philadelphia, Pa

"I've had the pleasure of speaking with Michael Rosman from the Corporate Caterer over the phone a number of times. He is very professional and really knows the corporate catering world inside and out.

He is a very warm and friendly guy! He is extremely approachable and spends as much time as needed on advice and tips. We have just begun our corporate catering division and I love the monthly PDFs he offers. I have printed out many of them and use them for reference. Michael's website was the launching pad I needed when I decided to move ahead with this division of my company. I'm so happy we found him and The Corporate Caterer. Thank you!"

-Davii Mandel
Mi Chicas Catering & Events
Spring Valley, NY

"I ended up hiring Michael to help create an operations manual for my catering operation, and things took off from there. Now, we have systems, formulas and procedures for everything. My one-year subscription paid for itself with our very first catering order!"

-K.S. Dewey
Dominoes Pizza
Bethesda, MD, New York, NY, Philadelphia, PA

"Michael Rosman has the perfect mix of knowledge and real world experience. I could tell he really listened to my concerns because he asked all the right questions and helped me define my goals. His coaching membership has given my catering division a clear focus and plan."

-Yasmin Tyebee
Top Nosh Café, San Jose, CA

"As an experienced operator, I did not expect to have so many "Aha! moments" as I read through all the material. I only wish I had found you a long time ago."

-Marsha Gayle
Providence, Rhode Island

"Michael is clearly an expert in corporate drop-off catering. It's one thing to read articles or books how-to grow your business. But when you have one-to-one consulting with someone with 30 years of experience – there is no better teaching tool. His consulting services have paid for itself many times over."

-M. Lindsey
The Duck Truck, Kingstown, NY

I am helping to grow a catering division in a family's restaurant. Having no prior experience in catering sales, I needed help. My search stopped when I found Michael's website. I ended up printing the pages and putting them in a 3-ring binder. I refer to it almost daily.

Later, I signed up for his consulting services. Michael is very knowledgeable and professional consultant. He listens, gives great advice and lots of encouragement. He helps me avoid many. I am more confident each time we have a discussion. It's been only three months, but I am already bringing in new business, and feel that I am moving in a right direction.

Iryna Zaritsky
Catering Sales Manager
MGM Roast Beef Catering

Made in the USA
San Bernardino, CA
29 February 2016